Works & Days

Winner of the 2010 T. S. Eliot Prize

The T. S. Eliot Prize for poetry is an annual award sponsored by Truman State University Press for the best unpublished book-length collection of poetry in English, in honor of T. S. Eliot's considerable intellectal and artistic legacy.

Judge for 2010: Claudia Keelan

WORKS & DAYS

DEAN RADER

Truman State University Press
New Odyssey Series

Cover art: "Desk," by Devon OpdenDries/Getty Images.

Type: Minion Pro © Adobe Systems Inc.; Arial © The Monotype Corporation
Printed by: Thomson-Shore, Dexter, Michigan USA

Library of Congress Cataloging-in-Publication Data

Rader, Dean.
  Works & days : poems / by Dean Rader.
    p. cm. — (New odyssey series)
  "Winner of the 2010 T. S. Eliot Prize."
  Includes bibliographical references.
  ISBN 978-1-935503-08-8 (alk. paper) — ISBN 978-1-935503-09-5 (pbk. : alk. paper)
  I. Title. II. Title: Works and days.
  PS3618.A3476W67 2010
  811'.6—dc22

                                                                      2010030705

The paper in this publication meets or exceeds the minimum requirements of the American
National Standard for Information Sciences—Permanence of Paper for Printed Library Materials,
ANSI Z39.48–1992.

For Jill & Gavin

What is the best thing for a man to ask of the gods in prayer?
—Hesiod

The self is not continuous.
—Kathy Steele

Art must fit with other things; it must be part of the system of the world.
—Wallace Stevens

Contents

Works

Traveling to Oklahoma for my Grandmother's Funeral,
    I Write a Poem about Wallace Stevens..................................3
Frog and Toad Confront the Alterity of Otherness........................6
How to Buy a Gun in Havana...9
Reading Yeats' "The Second Coming" on January 1, 2001..................12
Self Portrait: Blizzard...13
Hesiod in Oklahoma, 1934..15
Self Portrait: Rejected Pop Song......................................17
Self-Portrait: Equation...18
Einstein..19
Motherwell..21
Song for the Shell Shaker...22
PowerPoint Presentation on "The Sonnet"...............................24
The First Poem..25

&

The Poem You Ordered..28
Frog Loses Sleep Puzzling over Parallel Universes.....................29
Talking Points [Love Poem]..32
A Map of Unfinished Love Poems..33
    [elegy]..33
    [comedy]...33
    [haiku]..35
    [epistolary]...35
Self Portrait: Rejected Inaugural.....................................36
Self Portrait: Hesiod in Iraq...38
Self Portrait: Frank O'Hara to the Distended Angel....................39
Self Portrait: India to Texas...41
Self Portrait: One on One with Ezra Pound.............................43
Corrido for the Lost Girls of Juarez..................................44
Love Poem in 5 Couplets + 1 Line......................................45

Contingency Triptych: Three Self Portraits 46
    As Dido to Aeneas 46
    As Robert Hayden to Michael Jackson 46
    As Hesiod to Dorothea Lange....................... 46
While Looking Up the Etymology of "Country"
    in the *OED*, I Come Across "Cornucopia"......................... 48
[   ] 50
Frog Seeks Help with Anger Management 53

Days

Ocean Beach at Twilight: 14 56
Self Portrait at 30 57
On Reading Miguel Hernandez at 31, the Age of His Death 59
Self Portrait as Antinomy: 32 62
Reading Charles Wright in the Year of the Dragon: 33.................. 64
The Last Day of 34 65
What This Is: 35 67
Journal Entry on Love: 36 68
Self Portrait: Prayer at 37................................... 69
Frog and Toad Sing the Birthday Blues: 38..................... 70
Waking Next to You on My 39th Birthday or The Other Arm 71
Partial Elegy for the Self at 40............................... 73
Ocean Beach at Twilight: 41 74
    Kyrie 74
    Gloria 74
    Credo 75
    Sanctus 75
    Agnus Dei 76
    Ite Misse Est...................................... 76

Notes 77
Acknowledgments 79
About the Author 83

Works

Traveling to Oklahoma for my Grandmother's Funeral, I Write a Poem About Wallace Stevens

I

Early October and in Hartford,
The leaves leave on their orange parkas.
Winter sidles up like a bad salesman.

Section 14 of Cedar Hill Cemetery.
The grass, autumn-flecked, stubbles
Up: *the uncut hair of graves.*

Twenty-three days from now,
A maple leaf will unzip and
Head to the hard world below

Lighting on the ground about seven feet
Above the darkening body of Wallace Stevens:
Fat man, terrestrial, invisible as a god.

II

October on United Airlines flight 5481, seat 7C.
I am traveling to Oklahoma for my grandmother's funeral,
But all I want is to write a poem about Stevens:

The porch of spirits lingering, the grave in Hartford
Where he lay. My grandmother lies on a table
In the Southland Funeral Home in Tulsa.

Her body flies out of her body at an astonishing speed,
As though with purpose or direction, like an airplane
funneling home inside some great blue tube of sky.

Like everything else, we are in transit. We all sail
Toward the ocean of the dead, land of unknown arrival
And itinerary. Who is it that plans the schedule of ghosts?

III
The priest attending to Stevens
During his final days in the hospital,
Swears he made a deathbed conversion

To Catholicism, a claim his daughter denies.
I deny him nothing. It is cold in Connecticut.
The heavenly palms and bright green wings

Of Florida might as well be in Ceylon or Esthonia.
Is it possible that in the dissolving moment,
Stevens asked something of the God he believed

Might be a poem, or a woman skating? Who
Is to say that God took him seriously? At what
Point does the believer become the believed?

IV
The elderly woman next to me
In 7D has been peeking at this poem
For several minutes.

I don't mind,
Because the next line is this:
She will die before I do,

As will the man two rows in front
In 5C and his wife in 5D. But then again,
All of us on the plane could get there

In seconds. In the reverse burial that is this sky,
We die forward into the nothing that is not yet revealed.
We are the fading Stevens: we have no idea what lies ahead.

V

I wake and realize it's October 2, Stevens's birthday.
In Oklahoma, the red dirt goes on being red—
The dogwoods, the willows, the beige bony wheat stubs:

The riven days of wind: the sky like a drive-in screen:
The sky like an empty page: the sky like an underground sea.
Take me down, I say out loud, in this soft silver coffin.

It's the other world I want right now. But Oklahoma spools
On below. What I need is to ask my grandmother—
Her entire life a believer—if, in that flash of black light,

In that dissolving instant, she had the opposite doubts
Of Stevens; if she renounced the supreme fiction, the emptiness
Suddenly so clear, beyond the dividing and indifferent blue.

Frog and Toad Confront the Alterity of Otherness

The sun was hot in the sky
like a muffin in a bright blue tin.

The day was just the day.
The wind was nothing more

than wind, the leaves were leaves
and kept on being leaves.

Frog, however, wondered why
he was Frog and Toad was Toad.

Frog knew who he was,
but this strange morning

he feared he was the wrong one.
His skin felt too clammy,

his eyes too bulgy.
Even his pajamas seemed

that of another creature.
Everything was wrong:

the trees overhead; the birds in them.
Toad, on the other hand,

woke up troubled by how
different he was than Frog.

To him, Frog, was wholly
unknown and unknowable.

The yellow flowers outside his window,
the waterbirds down by the lake

that arrived only in winter,
the dreams of alligators and snakes

that swam through his sleeping,
all made more sense to him

than this Frog in his threadbare
suit and flappy feet.

How odd they both wanted to fold
into the foreign skin of the familiar,

inhabit the Frog and Toadness
of the other—

It is Toad who will understand
to love the unknown is to say yes

to the ineffability of difference.
And Frog shall find himself

stunned with a recognition
that to love the miasma of mystery

is to say yes to sorrow,
yes to the presence of absence,

yes to the chance that *alethia*
may never rise out of the pond.

Frog makes Toad some toast
with strawberry jam.

He waddles across the room,
sets down the plate,

pours Toad a cup of coffee.
The sun is hot in the sky

like a scone on a sky blue table.
Toad looks over at Frog.

Good old Frog, he thinks.
That bastard knows I hate toast.

Toad spreads the jam like a man
might smooth mortar on a brick

for which there is no building.
Thank you, he says,

Thank you Frog.

First, never say the word *gun*.
    Or *pistolero* or *buy*.

Talk instead about *platanos*. And smile.
    You'll know the bodega;

it's the one in Los Sitios with the wooden
    parrot clipped to the wire on

the left side of the door. When the wind
    springs up off the sidewalk,

the parrot bobs slightly, banging its crimson
    head against the building's wooden slats.

Go inside. On the far wall above the shelves
    of candles and tilty stacks of shirts,

you'll see the blackboard. It's the
    same in every store: an inventory

of *frijoles negros, arroz,* and *leche de coco,*
    menued in chalk. You will

scan the inventory for *platanos,* hoping
    they are in stock. You never know.

You will have brought with you
    a pouch of powdered milk. Inside

will be powdered milk and eight hundred
    fifty Euros. No dollars. No sterling.

The pouch will be glued shut. No tape. No
    staples. You will, as you do with

your wife, your children, your boss, barter.
    There is no baby formula in Cuba;

no cow's milk. You will hand over
    the pouch and ask for *platanos*.

It is said that at a similar bodega in Vedado,
    you look the man behind the counter

in the eye. But here, you are supposed to settle on
    the framed photo of the Catedral

de San Cristobal nailed to the wall above
    the shirts. The woman will place the

platanos in a plastic bag. You will take them.
    You will not say thank you.

No one knows the precise chain of events,
    not even you, because, as you are told,

you turn away. You walk over to the shelves
    next to the old Coke cooler and ruffle

through Frisbees, pantyhose, and postcards of
    Che playing golf in army fatigues.

By the time you are finished, your bag of
    platanos will feel *heavy*. At that point,

you walk out of the store, and out
    of Los Sitios, and make your way to

the Malecón, and you gaze at the lovers lounging
　　on the wall and you stop

for mango ice, and you ask yourself,
　　as you have done with everything

meaningful in your life, *what happens now?*

Reading Yeats's "The Second Coming" on January 1, 2001

To begin, to start out, to turn. To expand: to center and to throb.
To fall apart. To eat in the dark grammar. To spiral and to *oh*; to if.

To ask of the tantrum wind. To labor, to invoke bone, to anoint. To vex:
to wish, to want and to want. To will. To waste. To plug time's stoma.

To unfasten and to abandon. To erect: to shutter. To bleed. To unbuckle
the sprung sun. To plummet. To thigh. To saddle venom's gleam and to ride.

To limn or fringe. To regret the angel. To rivet. To say *riddle, substrate, alter*.
To rise the way bodies rise: to succumb: to chisel. To slit or suture; to slash.

To compress the ferric. To loose, to halo, to burn and congeal: to splinter.
To eat syntax in reverse, to limn wind's stoma, to saddle gleam, to ride venom.

To auger. To hear *whelp, seraphim, imago*. To leaden and live. To shiv, to sin.
To rend—to rip the gyre. To aport, to absess, to abseil. To apprehend.

To write *born, Bethlehem, beast*. To erase *palm, coffin, corpse*. To taper down.
To begin, start out, turn. To anoint bone, to rivet dark grammar. To slouch.

Self Portrait: Blizzard

Dropping from the sky
like flakes of soap,
big heavy chunks
like frozen leaves
or pieces of poems.
Dropping like wings of small birds
like thick onion skins
that freeze their own tears,
like bits of alabaster flesh
searching for bone,
like sugar cubes or lily petals,
like clumps of feathers or dandelions:
crumbs of white bread,
the dust of clouds:

Snow falls because it cannot rise,
cannot bend its knees,
or spread its wings.
It has no arms and cannot
climb the thin threads
it leaves streaming from the sky.
The more it falls, the more
it remembers its absence of rising.
To descend is not to ascend.
And not to ascend is to fall.
And to fall is to lose.

Snow is tired of losing.
Snow wants to watch TV on Sunday.
It wants to hibernate in the
winter, wear glasses
and put on a tie.
Snow wants to learn to tell time.

Snow wants to eat barbeque ribs,
and listen to Elgar,
it wants to kiss a man or a woman.
Snow wants to wonder about God.

It so happens that
Snow wants to be rain:
it wants to lounge on leaves
in the green of spring.
Snow wants be made love in,
sliding down buildings or bodies.

It wants to plunge on alfalfa and
corn stalks, and sound like a slap.
But Snow also wants ocean.
Snow is ready for water.
Snow wants to keep flowing.

But April beaten back like a shoreline,
leaves Snow to dream
of Rangoon, San Tropez, Antigua,
where it can take off its fuzzy coat
and return to the source of its making.

But Snow wakes to its work,
diving down on linens
left out on the line,
landing on underwear and tank tops,
where it melts into big
dirty drops salty as tears.

Hesiod in Oklahoma, 1934

They are simply, by god's inscrutable will, inferior men.
—H. L. Mencken on the dust bowl farmers

There is always the grass ahead of him on and on:
            and behind the grass the gouged skin they strip it from:

salt-spiked and silty, endless and unending:
            their labor the field's body, the field's body their stale host.

Lips blasted by sun and sand-sting: fissured fingers,
            broken and bloody gums, tongues leaden and drought-split:
and still they swallow the promise of redemption:
            they take it all on: thistle and wafer mash, dry-shod, dirt-devil

hoecake, and tumbleweed: the entire world parched as a rag:
            even the sky can't stop drinking: and still they dig:

venture their contract, venture their only covenant:
            empire never exhales, never slouches against plow

or pickaxe: neither apprehension nor acquittal,
            only acquisition, the slow accumulation of emptiness,
a revolving horizon of punishing absence, a sketchbook
            of space God left blank. And still, no one sees him

among the shades shoveling in the field, lonely farmer
            stooped and sullen but swift of hand:

strip to sow and strip to plough and strip to reap: this is the law of the plains.
            In Oklahoma, the plains beget the manna of scorpion

and grasshopper, the crushing tides of bluestem and grama
            parting for no man or magic stick: heavens hissing with

insect and electric, static of dust magnetic and mammoth.
          Stunned by gutted ground turned sky, Hesiod slings

a shovel over his shoulder, wanders in savaged sandals
          and straw hat among the troughs and crumbled dugouts

like one who has at once made and lost his own grave.
          That man is happy and lucky who does his work without

offending the deathless gods who discern the omens. What transgression,
          he wonders, what defect of composition, turns earth
against earth? tenant against host? the earliest endeavor of renewal
          and resurrection. Tired Hesiod: battered and bone-beat

Hesiod: pilgrim to emptiness and futility: pilgrim to the draperies of ash and
          topsoil: solitary witness to the apparition of work done,

lone pilgrim to the shrine of work undone. Find him unmoored among
          the sod huts and buried fences, among distances undulate and
unforgiving, sun-shot and shadowless: find him among toil and industry:
          find him kneeling over the long lines of the prairie

furrowed and famished: find the poet swathed in dirt: inscrutable and silent:

Self Portrait: Rejected Pop Song

I am not the songbird
I am not the devil's bunghole
I am not the oyster in the child's mouth
I am not the shantih, not the shantih

You are not the garden
You are not the world, not its children
You are not hell's glockenspiel
You are not the dictionary

Don't tell me you're the magic membrane
Don't tell me you're the ___, the ___
Don't tell me you're the hand job
Don't tell me you're the glove box heaven

Just tell me you're the soul ship
Just tell me you're the mouse ears
Just tell me you're the asschord, the asschord
Just tell me you're the *si se puede*

No one is the underbelly
No one is the mystic's nipple
No one is the White House homeslice
No one is the barber's sorrow

We are the woofer
We are the how to
We are the logos, the logos
We are *this* the

Self Portrait: Equation

Lesson: Let b be equal to the sum
of cosine and axefall—
unless the quotient of belief ÷ lightning
{or the insphere of trespass, skin-spark, and elegy}
shunts the heart's square root.
Existence is subtraction: even
time sloughs history's bruise.
    Mutatis mutandis.

Lesson: let x be your worst fear,
what you know divides you from you—
change y to *absence* and z to *fissure.*
Carry the remainder
in your pocket's tiny abacus.
    Lesson: all transformation is addition.

Einstein

The universe (which others call the Library)
—Borges

He hated tomatoes
And was afraid

Of the noises in the
Desert at dusk.

At times, the numbers
Thumped across the brain

Like horses or bad sentences.
Just a second of peace,

He would say to himself.
A moment

To see images, music, colors.
The calculus of the visible.

———————

What does it mean to see light
And think of a poem?

To see numbers
And arrive at heaven?

To look at stars
And picture a river?

What does it mean to know time
The way one knows a language?

To say that centuries or seconds
Are the letter *t* in a poem of infinite metaphors?

———————

If you divide the present by the past
You arrive at perception.

If you see light as wave,
You hear the word *silence.*

If you see light as particle,
You hear the word *wind.*

Is the opposite
Of darkness, darkness?

———————

Einstein thinks:
I know that what we are,

We have become, and what
We have become we turn

To shadow, and what the shadow
Touches, the present forgets.

Memory is the shadow of the present
Stretching backward

Forming the equation
To prove Borges was right:

God is a book.

The translator: me.
The language: desire.

If the body were not a canvas:

The brush would not be mistaken
For a penis or rain or loss.

And the light that rises
From the mouths of the dead

Would not seem like
Colors falling from the body

Of the canvas of loss.
But if the canvas is rain,

Then the brush of the body
Is the dead's elegy

To the other side of color.

Song for the Shell Shaker

The stones in the hills outside Durant
                                        silence the evening,
but so do those
                    in the river near Nanih Waiya.

Tonight, even the wind is weary.

Its sandy shoes scuff up the cedar limbs:
battered body
                    on a secret mattress.

Abandoned, invisible
                            the wind stopped
believing in God long ago,
                                or maybe
it was just yesterday,
or the moment before this poem.

Maybe it was the day when something passed
                                            between the woman
and the words she spoke,
a private understanding
                            like the silent nods of the blind:
a wind that blows
                    through the winds themselves.

Or maybe it was when the wind rose from its black bed
pushing the river rocks
                            toward memory of ocean,
And the stones in the hills
                            toward premonition of river—

turning within as the spheres might turn.

Sediment drum:
    stick of water:

stand in the silent music of the mound.

PowerPoint Presentation on "The Sonnet"

[14 lines]

[begin octave]

- The Earl of Surry composed the first sonnets   [Henry Howard, 1517–1547 British]
- in the English language. *Sonnet* comes from *suono,*
- the Italian word for *sound.* The sonnet reflected
- God's *order.* Frog heard that the name of the Hebrew   [⇐ this is a quatrain]

[STANZA BREAK]

- God could not be spoken. It makes Frog wonder: [children's books, see "Toad"]
- If that god made a poem of his name, could he read   [slant rhyme: read/Toad]
- it aloud? *Cantante Domino* Toad always says. That Toad… *[Latin "the domino sings"]*
- Hey, Frog exclaims, *God* and *Toad* sort of rhyme!

[STANZA BREAK]
[begin volta (Italian for "the turn") & sestet]

- *He is a fool which cannot make one sonnet,* says Donne.   [John, *metaphysical*]
- *And he is mad which makes two.* Frog contemplates   [tercet]
- this as he hops over to the pond. Peers in.   [another slant rhyme. Tedium?]

- His other self stares back from the tablet   [No couplet! Petrarchan]
- of the water's surface. *Take me to you,* it says to Frog.   [(1304–1374) Italian]
- *Blow, burn and make me new. Make me,* it whispers, *Make me.*

The First Poem

looks nothing like this—
    claws rust-stained and

blood-licked, its forehead
    flat, fear-flaked and riven.

It rose like some creature
    (we can't imagine

having to imagine)
    out of sump and sun-string.

Absence before absence,
    silence within silence:

muse of the tarred fire:
    muse of the stooped and woolen:

muse of the pre-angel, pre-god:
    don't just sing; split us open.

&

The Poem You Ordered

Once upon a time, you ordered a poem. You were considering throw pillows, a new ferret, or a hatchet, but a poem had been on your mind for months. You were finally ready to pull the trigger.

As for the details, you were certain what you wanted: something longer than a hammer; simpler than Sudoku. On the pull-down menu, you selected *quatrains* but then, after much deliberation, you changed your order to *couplets*. You paid extra for the stirrups, the tattoo but said no to the eye patch, the hammock, and all warranties.

You were tempted to ask for rhyme (it was included), but in the end, you declined. For you, it was all about story, and you worried rhymes would detract from the poem's *flow*. If it contained people, all the better: you preferred a tailor, the Russian woman from the bakery down the street, and your grandfather on your mother's side. But, you said to yourself, who gets everything?

As for the title, you chose the option *Surprise Me*.

Most of all, you thought, the poem would have to be about mercy, which would, of course, encompass loss. It must address war, and it must be open to closure. You didn't need *controlling metaphor*, and you had no interest in splurging for *metonymy*.

There is no anticipation like waiting for the poem you ordered to arrive.

When the poem you ordered ambled up the walk, you were caught off guard by the limp but nothing else—not its body cleaved in two, not the cowlick, not the delicate accretion of its form. You asked for this poem because for you, beginnings are never enough. It has always been about the ending.

To the window, foggy with your breath, you admit that you were never actually surprised by the limp. You knew the gun in the poem's pocket was loaded, and you knew where it was going. You had, after all, ticked the box marked *bullet*.

Frog Loses Sleep Puzzling over Parallel Universes

It was not the fear of nightmares or starchy sheets
that pulled Frog from his bed into night's exhale
where out on the grass in front of his house,
he fixed his attention on everything skyward.

The heavens ratcheted up, click by click.
Every puncture of brightness looked to Frog
like stickpins on the inside of a black balloon.

This idea made him think of a giant Frog
with a long silver beard. Maybe a cane or a robe.

The space between the sky and grass
was dark and deep. There was no wind.
Cricket under the porch was at it again, and Toad
fuzzy in his blanket, slept as only Toads sleep.

The sky notched again and snapped into place.
It had never looked bigger.
Frog thought of each star as a lily pad bobbing along
in the cosmos, and he wondered if there might be more frogs
beyond the starlight, hidden in the dark pools of sky,
distant tadpoles deep beneath the surface of the lake.

He imagined a crazy planet of Frogs
with six legs and pointy ears.
Frogs with pouches and sideburns
who drove around in green bumpy cars.
Frogs with two tongues who hated water.
Frogs with wings and hairy backs.

Frog had been reading again.
Heisenberg and Schrödinger made his head throb.

He knows electrons can be in two places
concurrently, but did that explain why
he wanted sleep and fly pudding at the same time?
Frog understands if he accepts cosmic inflation and
the holographic bound that parallel universes
are a hop away—an identical copy of this world
might only be 10^{100} meters from his still-warm bed.

But that was not what kept him awake.
It was the other worlds that drew him down.
He imagined a planet where Toad was a ballet dancer,
and one where Toad brought him tea with lemon
every morning. He thought about a world
in which Toad wears silly hats and capes
and another where Toad was 27 feet tall.
He loved the one where Toad only spoke Spanish,
the universe where Toad agreed with everything Frog said.
Toad, it's spring. Wouldn't you like to go for a walk?
Sí, Señor Frog. Este es una idea más excelente.

The night sky ticks on. Vast as it is, thinks
Frog, somewhere the balloon is tied off.
With the holographic bound, matter and energy
inside the sphere are limited to finite configurations.

This gives Frog hope that no world exists
where Toad never goes for swims,
or one in which Toad refuses to tell stories
when Frog is sick. He says out loud to no one that
he does not want to live in a world
where Toad is not his best friend.
Nothing moves, not the water, not the leaves, nothing.

The silence is broken by Badger and
Field Mouse who nod their heads toward Frog
as they shuffle off into night's back room.
In one of the worlds, the trees or the reeds

would respond to Frog,
but in this one, everything above is hushed.
The stars' lids never close. They
are as bright as they are silent.

This is what we have, says Frog.
Even if the wave function collapses,
  we still have this.
Siempre, tenemos este
* y verdad el otro,*
verdad el otro.

Talking Points [Love Poem]

- And the way the light crawls up the side of the sky at dawn;

- the room [the sky] when you open the curtains after a long morning in bed;

- the sun splashing on the sheets [*a bowl of lightning*];

- a flame: your face: the palms of Jesus in an El Greco painting;

- and the way the stars in their wool coats shine inward;

- the time I drew back your blouse [&] [kissed the light of your skin];

- the light crashing down your spine;

- the light curving [off] the curve of your hip;

- the light from the _____, the light in your mouth;

- the light on your body that says [*this way*];

A Geneology of Unfinished Love Poems

[elegy]

I don't know
what the dead
_____ about love,

if, for instance,
they remember it
the way an amputee

recalls a missing _____—
a necessary part
of the body found

only in a memory
of _____ slick
in water, hot

over flame, delicate
on thigh, in a mouth—
or if the ____ is just sorrow.

[comedy]

Your eyes are so _____.
There is no way
they can be glass,
though the left one

is always a bit
off center.

I wonder if your body
is already on the lookout
for the first _____
of my ear hair.

Your feet are so _____,
I don't care that they're webbed.
You're my duck.
My beautiful little duck.
You can't imagine the ways
I want to _____ you quack.

And then there is your _____.
_____!
I really like it.
In fact, I wish
I could carry it
around in my knapsack.
I'd _____ it the way
an archeologist
handles a sacred vase,
the way a cop grabs
the most dangerous felon.
I'd handcuff it to my belt loop.
I'd wear it like it was
Two loaded _____.

With the _____ union
even holy men forget
it is God they _____

Dear _____,

    I want to _____ for lying to you about that Home Ec. teacher. She meant nothing to me. And I need to come clean about the trapeze artist, the pool boy, your _____. What was I thinking?

    I hope you realize that I have forgiven you for pushing me into the _____ of that classics scholar. She's ancient history. That's a little joke, but I'm not joking about how _____ I feel: Your cousin Sophie. Really…my mistake.

    And about the palm reader. All she did was _____ my hand. Honest. But when she traced the creases, the narrow _____ on the map of the future world, she made me think: I want to know you the way she knows these lines. I want you to _____ me the way she knows how to lie.

Self Portrait: Rejected Inaugural

The land was land before we were us.
Our regret, freshly cut, clumps in the front yard.

History, memory's buttonhole, needs a new suit:
Its shoes, scuffed and spit-shined, wait by the door.

We wear ourselves as though it means something,
As if identity's moustache and glasses were made

To order. We are who we show others we
Should be, at least this is what we told

Ourselves as we dragged our whiteness across
The plains. We are what God wants us to be,

At least, this is what God told us as we dragged
Our blackness along the field. We are what

Our treaties say we are, at least this is what
Our fathers told us as we dragged our redness

Into the forests. As we did that first day,
We walk out onto the yard in our bare feet.

Today, though, we keep the mower in the
Garage. It's raining and it is going to rain.

Today, we wait for the sun, sky's
Only coin, to drop itself into the slot

Of America's phone: we ask who might
Answer when the other millennium

Calls to check in. We reply as we did then:
Look in your window. We are whomever

We are when we answer that phone. We are
What we say into the silence on the other end.

We are, as we always have been, the little chain
That dangles from mercy's bulb. We are,

As we always will be, the bulb at the end
Of conquest's wire, at least that's what

The soldier told us as we touched the switch.
We are what we say we might be. We are

Neither invention nor anodyne. As we
Walk across the yard, we say to ourselves:

We are what God asked us to be,
But we know that's never been true.

We are who we ask to be us.

Self Portrait: Hesiod in Iraq

Take, for instance,
this secret—
                    wind-banked
and wound-washed:
                    a cartridge of words
          the dead load and lock and
                              load again:

                    Then the young heroes with their hands from the sea?

And take this province of accretion:
                              skin mapped, flagged,
               wired for hum and hush—

                              these phrases:
unbuckled and broken,
                    spread out among our rewards.

                    In what kind of matter is it right to trust in men?

          Everything ordnanced—

morning's drab holster
                    empty   empty   and   empty   again:

                              Of what effect are righteousness and courage?
Load up sounds the body makes:
                    shapes vowels twist the body into:

noun of the body: noun of the blood

                              What is the mark of wisdom among men?

Where the word ends
                    avulsion begins.

Self Portrait: Frank O'Hara to the Distended Angel

Rilke said angels are made

of all we have forgotten.

The DNA of mine:

math formulas, due dates,

every Dickens novel,

that list of names I never

~~remember to~~ pray for.

[O the lost shapes!

O the coil of lacunae!]

If only misplacement

were a form of offering—

the abandoned

a subconscious tithe . . .

O the girth! O my

distended angel!

Can time's exhaust

be our only companion?

The calendar's gutter

our lone salvation?

January burns; July thaws.

And December,

God's Post-it note,

sticks to nothing.

Self Portrait: India to Texas

We redraw
Those woven borders of the soul,
Map again some faithful, raw
Region of the spirit
—David St. John, "Study for the World's Body"

I

The trip from Dallas to Delhi
                    takes more than a year
by horseback.
Lumbering across the ocean is worse
                              than navigating the Thar Desert:
water everywhere:
hoof-logged and hide-soaked,
                    filling the nostrils,
sliding
        down mane and tail,

the distance:
                nothing but dunes of ocean;

mirages of the opposite of water.

Longer
        is the swim from
Corpus Christi to Calcutta.
The ship of the body,
                        blue in its sandy skin
turns toward the stars,
                    searching
for more than guidance.

II

No one has mapped
                the boundaries of cloud and body,
sky and soulcrush:

             worlds third and first:

torso scar: : :

III
Rio Grande: Ganges:
Indus: Brazos:

Pani: Water: Agua:

IV
The sun is a river,
And the wind is a river,
And the heavens are rivers,
And these words are a river.

And your eyes are a river,
And your hands are a river.
And your mouth is a river,
And your heart is a river.

I drink
Like a sailor
Thirsty for what
He can only imagine,

Or a man
Lifting a cup
Of something
Holy.

Self Portrait: One on One with Ezra Pound

And then went down the lane,
                    elbow to sternum, elbow
to jawbone, jawbone to chin,
                    spin and plant, spin, and
the key open as the blank page,
blank as a page opened on Christmas,
                    the gift thy free passage,
but Pound for whom sin comes sharp
                    comes hard,
     no dolphin faster in moving:
nothing is negotiable,
                    not the soon-to-be-striken, not the
gruel-hearted or star-stretched, and
no, not the clean lay-up,
                    not the bunny in the basket,
     the coin in the cup,
it's all vernacular:
                    the ten-armed ghost
swatting everything back—
                    hamadryas under the sun-beat:
even when the lane looks clear,
                    (legs anchored to the heavy planks,
whitecaps of hair
                    leagues in the distance),
he is Scylla,
          Charybdis
bad to swallow my mad drive to the rim,
badder to fling me
                    like a sea-soaked ship against the rocks,
but OY TIΣ doesn't work in the paint,
     and forget the warp and the woof:
O to carve a path
                    through the bumm drum

O light tensile immaculata—
                    here, error is all in the not done:

Corrido for the Lost Girls of Juarez

Of the men who take them we say:
If not in this world, then the next

Of the men who take them we say:
May the body you needed never be yours

Of the men who take them we say:
May your best moment come when your cock turns to dust

Of the men who take them we say:
May we find you before the devil knows you're dead

Love Poem in 5 Couplets + 1 Line

I want to know the word
For your back in the morning,

The noun for the sound you make
When my tongue goes along your breast,

The verb for my mouth
On yours.

The unknown language of bodies is vast.
Stacks of dictionaries around our bed

Are like the empty sheets
When you are away:

A symbol of what is missing.

Contingency Triptych: Three Self Portraits

I. *As Dido to Aeneas*

We wake: the night star-scorched & stained, morning fetal and uncoiling:
everything lifting: treehush and moondive: you at the window, the window

at day's limn. The day (heart's fulcrum) lists. Hear me: even if the bed
is an iron net, and the mattress a cage of twine and sawgrass: even if my legs

are bars and my arms are bars, the body's chain of sweat and skin
is no prison: it's the floating cell of the ship that will lock you down.

II. As Robert Hayden to Michael Jackson

And if the mirror asks nothing of the face
fixed in its gaze but a moment of clarity? To see
is to be seen, but to reflect is to enter that space
in which the self doubles down. Someone said let be
be the finale of seem, as though existence and
perception form the wishbone of knowledge.
Even the absent eyes blinking back understand
that breaking the bone is more than a hedge
against the delta of the seen versus the known.
We don't want the trope of skin as map or
mastery. Nor do we need to be shown
the body's secret body to know that the door
to the other opens inward: sight is more than mere
perception. To see is to look inside what we fear.

III. As Hesiod to Dorothea Lange

Sky, rumpled and shit-stained—

           not unlike so many things,
the human heart, for example,

         or God's workshirt:
mothballed and collar-ringed,

         stiff as a horseshoe. Discarded.

A cracked photo
                curls in the breast pocket: God giving the thumbs up.

Good times.

In the underworld, every soul has work,
                                even if it's the labor of dying.
No one has time to sit for pictures, not Judas,
                                not the devil,
though the latter can't stop smiling.

In heaven every angel is naked.
Their portraits, maps of transparency,
                                radiance reversed.

The celestial Graflex never needs a flash,
But that's why eternity is so expensive.
Down here
                we could use a little light.

From the clouds, the camera sees
little more than landscape:
                                a contact sheet of absence—
nothing but grid after grid of dejection.

And yet we pose in our dresses and suits
hoping the macro zoom centers us in the frame.

But what if the darkroom is empty?
                                No eye on the diaper of history?

What if there is no close-up?
                                No snapshot of rope burn or knuckle-scab?
Only the tremble that through the viewfinder
                                we are no longer watched.

While Looking up the Etymology of "Country" in the *OED*, I Come across "Cornucopia"

and I can't stop thinking about the pumpkin—
fat little soldier at the front of the platoon,
sentry to the tasteless vegetables that sound
the way they look: *squash*, for example, and *gourd*.

And I wonder what lurks behind
the phalanx of grapes, daisies, and apples;
the battalions of chestnuts, tomatoes,
lettuce, and pecans that tumble like wounded

bodies onto the field of bounty. What sacred
symbol of plenty hides inside the Trojan horse
of the horn? Secret fall berries or miraculous
autumn peach? You fill the hollow that hungry

Zeus must have found when he broke off the
horn of poor Amalthea—the Mary of Mount
Idi, forgotten Madonna, cloven-hoofed virgin—
holy goat mother to the history's other god:

Imagine the shame of being raised by a single
goat (everyone knows wolves and bears
make better parents. No girl wants to kiss the
goat boy, bolt of lightning or not). And so he lives

to fill the empty horn—sweet persimmon of Leda,
apricot skin of Hera, calendar of nectar, daily
cycle of tongue and lip, orchard of the forbidden—
which is why you never see a mango in a cornucopia

(or a papaya). No dates or figs or salty olives,
no kiwi or guava, only stringy melons and the waxy

skinned foods with cobs and shells to be used
as tools, edible brother to the busted horn—

O basket of bone, trumpet of keratin, O womb of
production and consumption, O ridiculous
cornucopia, metaphor for my country and
its solitary, stolen birth. Shrine of sawgrass

and wheat stalk, plentitude of the drab and
tasteless, you depend on the pumpkin,
America's worst food—swollen larval carrot,
retarded beach ball, cranium for God's rejected

lot—canonized by the cornucopia's halo. Sad pumpkin,
sorry seedy pumpkin, you make me want to know
what gifts await us in the other horn, what sweet fruits
were saved for us by the broken bitter gods.

No one could explain
    why the words went missing.

One day, during conversation
    over coffee, our brains pulled back

the drawer to get _____ from the
    files, but it was gone.

We felt there was a word for the
    emotion we wanted to express,

And yet, no one could locate it.
    We searched the cluttered desks

of our vocabularies, but nothing turned
    up. It was buried, lost, or both.

The next day, we couldn't find _____,
    the day after ____.

There were some who had not lived
    with the words so didn't feel the absence.

But for the rest of us, simple exchanges became
    more and more difficult;

worst was how we talked to ourselves
    about ourselves. The precision

of self-examination gave way to
    ambiguity. Everything became frustrating

in part, because we wanted that which
      that had left. We were like

a carpenter who reaches for a tool that has
      always hung from the same peg

but was suddenly missing, or a fisherman
      searching his tackle box for

just the right lure only to discover a blank
      space where the silver hook should be.

Induction revealed nothing. Our mental
      sleuthing uncovered _____.

The next week, seven more disappeared—
      and it wasn't just ____, as you

may have heard, but _____ and _____
      as well. It felt like part of

our bodies had been stolen. We miss
      the words the way an amputee

grieves the toe he rarely noticed, the finger
      he used only when holding a cup

or pencil. Even now, I wonder about this
      poem. We have learned to work

around the missing, but how long
      will that last? Will ____ in the future

come across these lines and find parcels of
      blank spaces, vacant lots between

the dilapidated houses, as though
  a hurricane ripped half of our

houses from their foundations.
  We ____, but so far, nothing.

And so we wait. We've invented new words,
  but, they are probably not the same,

which means that our world has changed. We
  are _____ people. And so we wait

either for someone to find the words
  or for the words to find us:

compass and sign, beacon and _____.
  It all hinges on this—we are what we speak.

Go ahead. Sit there in silence. We know it was _____.

Frog Seeks Help with Anger Management

It all began the morning Toad greeted him with *What up?*
Leave it to Toad to turn breakfast into performance.
But, then he forgot to TiVo *Dancing with the Stars*. Again.
You can picture the scene: a remote, a fireplace. A lava lamp,

a hurl. See glass and gloop shatter. See Toad and wall weep.
Rage is the mother of beauty, thinks Frog. But, tell that to Toad
who got punched for spilling beer in the fly pudding. See Toad
watch *Oprah*. See Toad pray for guidance. Hi God, it's me, Toad!

The ecstatic conquest of the awful leads to salvation. Just ask Jesus.
See the Christ's whipchord. See the Christ drive the tax-man from
the temple. Go ask Jesus about thaw and burn. Better yet, ask Frog

about the socket of desire. Woo-wee it's dark in there. See Frog want.
Rage is the stepson of ruin; the fuckbuddy of sorrow. See Toad deal.
See the peace that passeth. Tell Toad it's not about survival but resurrection.

Days

Who's to say the stars understand
their heavy labor, or the moon its
grunt work across the hard curve of absence?
Who's to say the gulls taut on their tiny strings

believe the air? Everything seems surprised
by the fat slab of pink strung up against the blue:
the dogs dark in night's water, the fishermen
buoyed to the beach's pillar of stillness.

Even the teenage boy playing in the spoor
of foam and backflow pauses longer
than expected, his father's voice dissolved

in the din-drop of surf and sea hush. Night
is no curtain. When he stares out across
the wave of waves, who's to say he looks inward?

Self Portrait at 30

Death flicks my ear
with his stubby finger

as he moseys out the door

and into the garden.
Fatty clouds, sticky

and white, roll along

like cakes on heaven's
blue conveyor.

He picks his teeth, Death,

and takes a pee behind
the bushes, winks at you.

The relic buried beneath

the elm is your shinbone.
Or maybe it's mine.

Caret initio et fine.

I'm wearing a hat
with a little propeller on top.

You are on your knees

near the back porch:
a spade in one hand,

a Twinkie in the other.

Even The End
has to end sometime,

says the Buddha.

Or was that the
neighbor lady peeking

over the fence?

No matter: my cupcake
only has one candle,

and the wind readies to rise.

On Reading Miguel Hernandez at 31, the Age of His Death

Don't tell me
The heart is a flower,
Opening and closing
Like a mouth
Swallowing daybreak.
Or even that it's
A candle,
Jerking its pulse
Toward God.

If life is this, I wonder what death would be.

Tell me instead
About the time
I searched
For his grave
Along the edges
Of Madrid,
Or when I found his corpse
Buried under a folded corner
Of Lorca's *Sonetos,*
Blossoming like a lover
Under spring stars.

Is this my grave or the womb of my mother?

Tell me again
About the letter
From his wife,
Received in prison:
No food for their son
But bread and onions.

And describe the tuberculosis.
The heaves
Of blood and stone,
Their ragged acquittals
Peeling away
The skin of his lungs
Like a knife
On his son's dinner.

I go on in the dark, lit from within.

And perhaps
You could remind me
Of the moment
I found him nailed
To my palms,
A forgotten criminal
Or god,
Unable to fall
Into the bottomless
Body of the next world.

Maybe I'm still waiting to be born.

Tell me
That the heart
Is more than
Burning bread,
More than
Crimson stone
At the edge of
The grave
Of the body.
Tell me
The heart
Is God's pulse
Pressing word

After word,
Into a poem
That awaits me
In your mouth.

Tell me that if I swallow it,
I'll go on
Lit from within.

I know what our father needed
        from our mother—fused
                brightness always

uncoiling. And her:
        the jolt of hurtle,
                charge of ambition:

internal polarity,
        of the unplanned,
                magnetism inscrutable.

Heredity, time's meter maid,
        never writes a warning—
                the laptop of history

never loses your name.
        Data in a vein of data.
                Centrifuge and swirl.

The gravity of the past,
        tugs us like some listing ship
                into electric seas—

watery genes you and I share.
        I wear our father's body,
                costume to a party

for which there is no invitation.
        Arrival is little more
                than interrogation,

so forgive me: because
     for you I have only
          questions: what

do you know of tomorrow's menu?
     What do you believe?
          What will you say to the child

you may never meet?
     What is it you cannot
          tell your husband?

There are more, but the one
     I always come back to: will
          this still world hum if you are

no longer its breath?

Reading Charles Wright in the Year of the Dragon: 33

Late July. June on all fours,
                              dug in.
It won't let go,
                  but neither will God.
Neither will the idea of God.

The human body is a leaf.
The soul,
          well, that's a different story…

Wright says, I find, after all these years, I am a believer.

I wrote the same line
in a stained notebook years ago,
But then again, who hasn't?
We write and erase,
                    write and erase…

We all fit in the flaming robe
                                the closer we come to Satan's mouth.

What we know:
We must live with language on fire.
We must speak through incineration.
There is no erasure,
                    only absence.

Eternity is simply the beginning,
                                  everything else is desire.

I want the opposite of desire,
I want to inhabit the other self,
I want to recline in the word *motion*,
I want the secret locked under God's fat tongue.

The Last Day of 34

I

Tomorrow when the sun
ladders up
        across the hooded blue,
I will slip into my 35th year:
                life's little bathroom break:
and then
       the trundle bed of the future:

Ia

Early morning sky, moonmapped
                for the sleeping traveler:
death's dreaming twin

II

What passages
       do we make alone?
And where do we go when we land there?

How strange to believe
           we journey from one year to the next.
How so like us to think we move *forward*.

If there are crossings,
        we believe we make them.
If there is solitude,
          we say *there are others*.

III

On that bridge,
       in that city in Switzerland,
you said
     community is work.

For all I know, God may be in both.

For all you know, God may be both.

####### IIIa
It was almost impossible to discern
the river from the sky:
                        the tidal darkness:
the people on the promenade:
the bridge
            from the water.

####### IV
It is the evening
                before my 35th birthday,
and I am standing on a bridge in San Francisco.

One year ago, we traveled
                        from Switzerland back to Paris.
We drank champagne on your balcony.

It was the evening of my 34th birthday.

I remember nothing else of that day
except the sky,
                which comes back only now
as I look out over the city:
                        it's that hazy blue,
the jacketed deepness
that keeps
            sneaking along the horizon,
heading toward the color
                    of some other person's memory.

####### IIb
We want so much.

####### IIc
We only believe
                in what we ask for.

1. This is the vase for the flowers you're holding
2. This is the sign on the wall that I'm gone
3. This is your chance to create a distraction
4. This is the answer to 7 across
5. This is the heaven we can't reimagine
6. This is the hammer this is the chain
7. This is not at all what you asked for
8. This is the way we do things in Russia
9. This is something quite different from that
10. This is my body that lies down in darkness
11. This is the word spoken aloud
12. This is not what I thought would happen
13. This is the heart and this is the heart
14. This is the part of the poem you wanted
15. This is my hand it's touching your elbow
16. This is the language we all have to use
17. This is the same thing we did in the morning
18. This is the question I won't ever ask
19. This is the place you can take me for coffee
20. This is the dog that misses his tail
21. This is for keeps it can't be returned
22. This is my penance for all of my _____
23. This is perhaps the craziest line
24. This is forever, that is for now
25. This is the tree I planted in Cypress
26. This is the place on your thigh that I'll kiss
27. This is the one I've been talking about
28. This is the light that is absent of shadow
29. This is all I can do for you now
30. This is the lie that I'll tell you tomorrow
31. This is the heart and this is the heart
32. This is the reason we choose to believe
33. This is the word we know never to say
34. This is not over it's hardly begun

We say it is the wand in life's hand
we say it is the pigeon
                the rabbit even
tucked away inside fate's black hat

but love is the guillotine
the flung knife
                the body chained in a casket of water

it is the magic coin in the child's ear
the folded dollar
                that appears in the pocket of your coat
the queen of hearts torn
                    to pieces and taped back together

Self Portrait: Prayer at 37

I want to ask
for nothing

but the little boat
in my heart

lifts its anchor
and sets out:

by *nothing*
I mean *everything*:

the ocean I
float in

the life vest
just out of reach.

No one spreads your butter like Toad.
 His heart is jelly, his tongue is jam.
He'll nibble the crust right off of your bread.
 Give him your fruitcake, and he'll give you his ham.
No one spreads your butter like Toad.

No one pumps your engine like Toad.
 He'll coax you slow or rev you fast.
He'll be the pickup, you be the bed—
 His hand the throttle, your body the gas.
There's no one pumps your engine like Toad.

No one knows your toolbox like Toad.
 He can loosen a nut or tighten a cog.
He'll fasten your trim, he'll even bring wood,
 But for bigger equipment, you have to call Frog.
For the biggest equipment, you better get Frog.

Waking Next to You on My 39th Birthday
or The Other Arm

The bed we share is a ship.
You are the captain
                                in a big blue hat.
We sail all night
                        like crazy Odysseus
thirsty for Penelope undressed on the shore.

I am the bearded sailor
                        who wants to take you below deck:

ropes, canvas, hooks:

The heavy sails above,
                        the heavy waters beneath.

Your bottom arm even heavier.
Your fingers turn purple,
and your hand,
                a helpless fin sinking in the darkness.

This bed of ours is the sea,
                                and I am a one-armed swimmer.
You wriggle up close like a dolphin.
You slide in next to me like a fish,
                                a small shark, maybe.
You are hungry, and I am trailing blood.

This bed of ours
                is a boat,
and with my only limb, I row us to shore.
The other, fast asleep under your back,
                                numb in its tingly case:
Hard,
        like the bottom of a hull

or the wooden slats of a frame.

It's always the same problem:
what to do with my other arm:

I'd like to unhook it at the shoulder,
and set it on the nightstand.
I could use it to scratch your back

                              or your feet,
all those places your fingers can't reach.

With me it's the left one,
you,
      the right.
We know the ritual:
your am slides under my neck,
you crawl onto my chest.
and for five minutes:

                  moss on rocks.

But then it happens,
                  the hot stings of the jellyfish
on forearm, in fingers.

We roll over into the vastness of covers, blankets,
and I am floating alone

                  on the world's smallest raft.
The waterbirds circle and keep circling.
I see you across the wide spread of distance.

This bed of ours is an ocean.
I could tread water until morning,

                  but we dive in to drown.

I want you to walk me out on the plank and push me over.

Like a severed anchor,

            I want to sink.

§   laid down among the ashes, an assignation
§   hands clasped and finger missing
§   *notation*: the silence we are forgotten into
§   paralysis of habit, rest stop of orthodox
§   axis rending and thus onward
§   *proposition*: there is no elegy
§   in this we are no more than the knelt
§   *question:* what gets to be beautiful?
§   fallacy of the long-under, fallacy of simile
§   listen: motion (not night) makes itself hollow
§   flicker, replica, invasion, skein
§   ravine: the exogenic
§   what he says (and then some)
§   *proposition*: is is construction
§   interstice of ~~the ordinary~~ psalm and retraction of psalm
§   lullaby for year zero ("Lemon Tree")
§   nothing is what it is
§   lament to mental as being to begin
§   *notation*: the abandonment of x into the thoughts one has about it
§   fingers clasped and hand missing
§   *question:* what gets to be finished?
§   entropy of the body [strike that]
§   here the sayable, here the interval
§   *proposition*: there is only elegy

Ocean Beach at Twilight: 41

—After Arvo Pärt's *Te Deum*

Kyrie

Unto the end, O lord,
                    unto the end.
            Drink up the darkness and
                                recommence this:
                    our unlocked hour.
        Night's measure:
                        caesura of distance and longing.
            The fat oboe of moon
                                quarter-notes the same sound;
        our hearts,
                    your little records,
stuck on the same prayer.

Gloria

    Who,
            if you were to cry out,
would hear you amidst the drown of
                            sea-crash and skin song?
            Down here
                    our skullcaps of malefact
            and washout
                    let nothing—
                                not excelsis,
    not the clock's fingersnaps,
                        not even your roll call—
            slip past our earbuds.

And the body,
> strung like a cello
>> across time's fingerboard
> believes in its own music, believes
>> in hammering through
the great rest:
> Score of vestige and lineament,
>> score of sun-scrim,
> score of mercy sought and mercy attained, we wait
> like singers struck dumb
>> for the final tenuto.

Undertow of strings.
> Coda our chorus
> back to this beached world.
>> Stars candle out across
> the sea of heaven—
>> waves metronome in,
> marking arrival and resurrection.
Twilight of the mortals
> doesn't have the same zip
> and yet, here you are,
>> lone pilgrim to absence and afterflow.
> Our voices
>> sing down the sun like they always have
>> and always will.
You ask again:
> what dark pit opens
>> beneath the ocean's fathomed stage?

[silence begets silencio]

O choir of exhumation,
> call me up.

He who comes before

        the great conductor,

    brings an offering

          of ossia and catgut.

                Miserere nobis, maestro,

      our instruments are out of tune.

Mercy's cup overturneth,

          as we overturn those whose sins we swallow:

    How do we tell dismissal

          from obstruction?

In the beginning, O lord,

        in the beginning:

    unlocked moon, caesura of exhumation.

                Our skullcaps strung

      like a violin of sun-scrim,

          our hearts drown in sea-crash

   and skin-song.

        Night's undertow and mercy's tenuto

          candle up into absence and lineament.

      Go, it is the dismissal:

Pilgrim of this beached world,

        recommence our hearts:

   vestige of mercy, record of

        longing and malefact,

             we sing up

     our fathomed prayer, our offering of silver and washout—

final music of obstruction

        and resurrection.

      O distance,

          O silent measure,

   drink down the body:

       drink down time's cup.

Notes

Traveling to Oklahoma for My Grandmother's Funeral, I Write a Poem about Wallace Stevens
Wallace Stevens, "Sunday Morning," "Of Modern Poetry," and "Notes toward a Supreme Fiction"

Frog and Toad Confront the Alterity of Otherness
The Frog and Toad poems take great liberties with characters from Arnold Loebel's fantastic children's books but do not contain any specific material—aside from the names of Frog and Toad—from Mr. Lobel's works.

How to Buy a Gun in Havana
For (but not about) Cristina Garcia

Self Portrait: Blizzard
Pablo Neruda, "Walking Around"

Hesiod In Oklahoma, 1934
Archibald MacLeish, *The Land of the Free*; Hesiod, *Works and Days*; and Edward Hirsch, "Orpheus Ascending" and "Nebraska 1883"

Motherwell
Robert Motherwell, *Elegy for the Spanish Republic,* in particular, *Elegy for the Spanish Republic #34, 1953–54.*

Song for the Shell Shaker
For Leanne Howe
"Nanih Waiya" is the central mound built by the Choctaw in Mississippi. Durant is the Choctaw capital in Oklahoma.

PowerPoint Presentation on "The Sonnet"
John Donne, "Batter my heart, three person'd God; for, you" and Wikipedia

Frog Loses Sleep Puzzling Over Parallel Universes
For Brandon Brown

Talking Points [Love Poem]
For Jill Ramsey

A Map of Unfinished Love Poems
For Mike Henry and Sonia Feher

Self Portrait: Hesiod in Iraq
The Contest of Homer and *Hesiod, 1914*

Self Portrait: One on One with Ezra Pound
Ezra Pound, "Canto I," "LVI," and "LXXIV"

Love Poem in 5 Couplets + I Line
Yehuda Amichai, *Selected Poetry of Yehuda Amichai*

While Looking Up the Etymology of "Country" in the *OED*, I Come Across
    "Cornucopia"
For Chris Haven, Brian Clements, Amorak Huey, Christina Olson, Mark
    Schaub, Todd Kaneko, and Brian Dempster

On Reading Miguel Hernandez at 31, the Age of His Death
Miguel Hernandez, "Sigo en la sombra, lleno de luz"

Self Portrait as Antinomy: 32
For my sister

Reading Charles Wright in the Year of the Dragon: 33
Charles Wright, "Ars Poetica II"

The Last Day of 34
For Sara Chapman

Self Portrait: Prayer at 37
Meghan O'Rourke, "Prayer"

Waking Next to You on My 39th Birthday or The Other Arm
For Jill Ramsey

Ocean Beach at Twilight: 41
Arvo Pärt, *Te Deum*

Acknowledgments

Thank you to those who read and commented on portions of this book: Cristina Garcia, D. A. Powell, Fred Marchant, Brian Clements, Chris Haven, Joan Houlihan, Jane Miller, Amorak Huey, Jonathan Silverman, Catherine Staples, Catherine Prescott, and LeAnne Howe.

I'd also like to thank Dean Jennifer Turpin and Associate Dean Peter Novak at the University of San Francisco for faculty development funds, writing retreats, and sabbatical release time that supported the completion of this book. I'd also like to thank my good colleagues in the English Department at USF and our fantastic students.

Thanks to Kelly Cherry for selecting "Hesiod in Oklahoma, 1934" for *The Sow's Ear Poetry Review* Poetry Prize and to Stacy Carlson, who picked "Frog Loses Sleep Puzzling Over Parallel Universes" for the *Crab Creek Review* Poetry Prize. A very special thanks goes to Claudia Keelan for choosing this manuscript for the T. S. Eliot Prize. I am truly indebted.

I would also like to acknowledge all of the editors and readers at the various journals who accepted these poems for publication—in particular Judith Taylor and Patty Seyburn at *POOL*. I am especially thankful to Nancy Rediger and Barbara Smith-Mandell, editors at Truman State University Press, and all of the dedicated folks at Truman who make this series happen.

Immeasurable thanks to my family—both immediate and extended—for everything. Most notably, my wife, Jill, and my son, Gavin, to whom the book is dedicated. Thank you also to Jill for her work with the cover design.

Lastly, thanks to the reader. In the end, there is only you.

Grateful acknowledgements to the following publications in which these poems—some with different titles and in slightly different form—first appeared.

Berkeley Poetry Review: "Reading Yeats's 'The Second Coming' on January 1, 2001" and "Self Portrait: Rejected Inaugural"
Borderlands: "Motherwell"
Cincinnati Review: "Self Portrait as Dido to Aeneas"
Colorado Review: "Frog Loses Sleep Puzzling over Parallel Universes"
Common Ground Review: "Talking Points [Love Poem]" and "Journal Entry on Love: 36th
Connecticut River Review: "Love Poem In 5 Couplets + 1 Line"
Connecticut Review: "How To Buy A Gun In Havana"
Crab Creek Review: "Frog and Toad Confront the Alterity of Otherness"
DMQ Review: "Self Portrait: Hesiod in Iraq" and "Self Portrait at 30"
Fire (UK): "The Last Day of 34" and "Self Portrait: Blizzard"
Harpur Palate: "Ocean Beach at Twilight: 41"
The MacGuffin: "The Poem You Ordered" and "While Looking Up the Etymology of 'Country' in the OED I Come Across 'Cornucopia'"
Oak Bend Review: "Waking Next to You on My 39th Birthday"
Parthenon West Review: "Reading Charles Wright in the Year of the Dragon: 33"
Poet Lore: "Ocean Beach at Twilight: 14"
POOL: "What This Is: 35," "Frog Seeks Help with Anger Management," "Frog and Toad Sing the Birthday Blues: 38," and "PowerPoint Presentation on the Sonnet," and "[   ]"
Quarterly West: "Geneology of Forgotten Love Poems" and "Self Portrait: Rejected Pop Song"
The Sow's Ear Poetry Review: "Hesiod in Oklahoma, 1934"
Salamander: "Self Portrait: Equation" and "The First Poem"
The Wallace Stevens Journal: "Traveling to Oklahoma for my Grandmother's Funeral, I Write a Poem about Wallace Stevens"
Veer: New Verse: "Self Portrait: India to Texas," and "Einstein"

"On Reading Miguel Hernandez at 31, The Age of His Death" and "Song for the Shell Shaker" appear on the innovative *Borderlands Web Audio Site.* My thanks to the many people behind this excellent project.

"Corrido for the Lost Girls of Juarez" is part of a large-scale art exhibit in El Paso, Texas, by artist Richard Kamler.

"Talking Points [Love Poem]" and "Journal Entry on Love: 36" received Honorable Mention in the 2008 *Common Ground Review* poetry contest.

"Frog and Toad Confront the Alterity of Otherness" won the 2007 *Crab Creek Review* Poetry Prize.

"Hesiod in Oklahoma, 1934" won the 2009 *The Sow's Ear Poetry Review* Poetry Prize.

About the Author

Dean Rader is professor of English at the University of San Francisco where he held the National Endowment for the Humanities Chair. He has published widely in the fields of poetry, literary studies, American Indian studies, and visual and popular culture. He has received the *Crab Creek Review* Poetry Prize (2007) and *The Sow's Ear Poetry Review* Poetry Prize (2009). He regularly contributes op-eds and book reviews to *San Francisco Chronicle* and blogs at *The Weekly Rader, SemiObama* and *52 Gavins*. A native of Weatherford, Oklahoma, he now lives in San Francisco with his wife and son.